FAB FOUR FRIENDS

The Boys Who Became the BEATLES

SUSANNA REICH

illustrated by ADAM GUSTAVSON

Christy Ottaviano Books

HENRY HOLT AND COMPANY ✦ NEW YORK

JOHN

On a dark October night in 1940, John Lennon was born in the mighty port of Liverpool, where the River Mersey meets the cold, salty sea.

England was at war with Germany, and baby John's cries were often drowned out by the wail of air raid sirens.

John grew into a handsome lad who giggled at Dad's silly jokes. Both of them were dazzled by Mum, with her long red hair falling in waves and her easy laughter.

Most of the time Dad was away at sea, and Mum would leave John with Aunt Mimi and go out dancing. If John woke from a bad dream late at night, Aunt Mimi would be there to comfort him. But it wasn't the same as having Mum.

After Mum and Dad split up, five-year-old John was sent to live with Aunt Mimi and Uncle George for good. The war was over, and nights were quiet. Uncle George sang nursery rhymes and tucked John into bed. "Give me a squeaker," George would say, and John would plant a noisy kiss on his cheek. Aunt Mimi baked apple tarts for John, tidied his room, and made sure he minded his manners.

Mum visited. But each time she left, John missed her terribly.

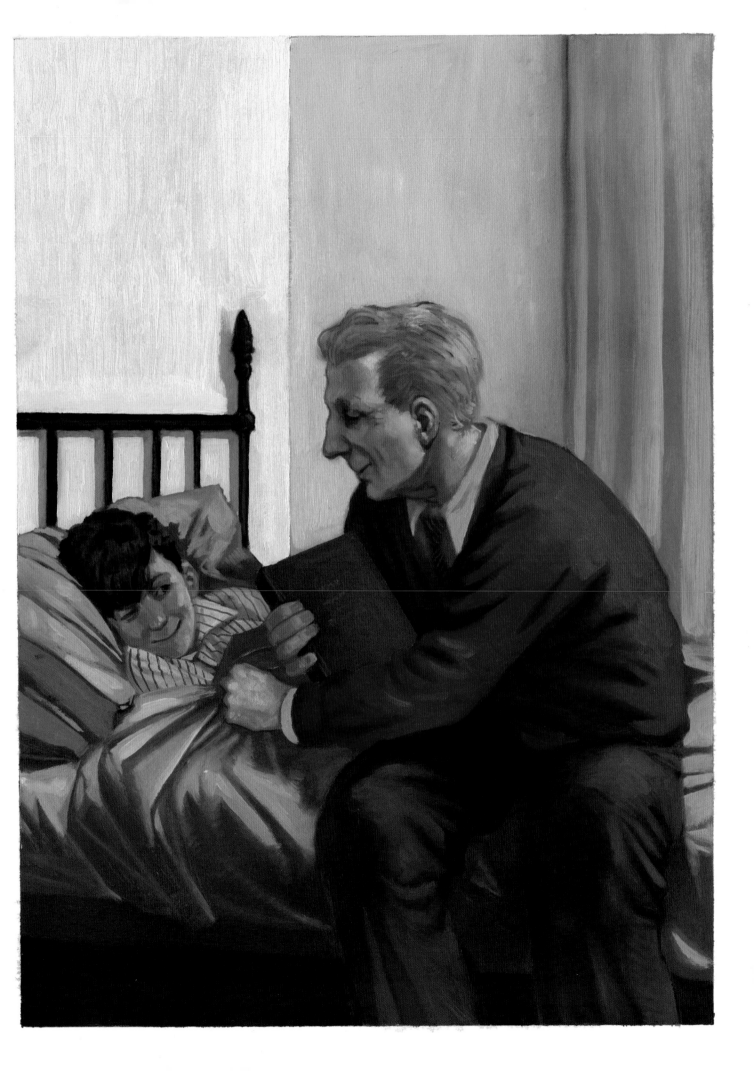

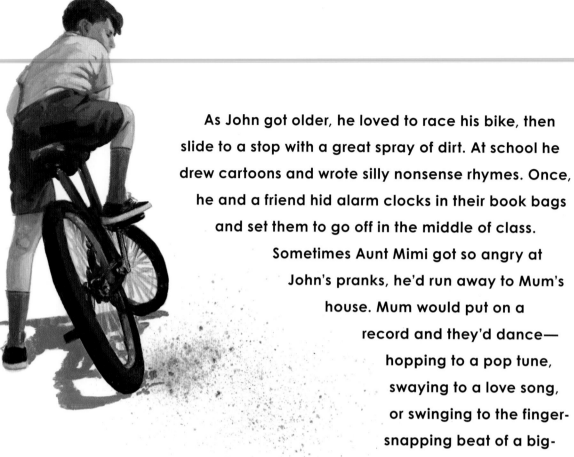

As John got older, he loved to race his bike, then slide to a stop with a great spray of dirt. At school he drew cartoons and wrote silly nonsense rhymes. Once, he and a friend hid alarm clocks in their book bags and set them to go off in the middle of class.

Sometimes Aunt Mimi got so angry at John's pranks, he'd run away to Mum's house. Mum would put on a record and they'd dance— hopping to a pop tune, swaying to a love song, or swinging to the finger- snapping beat of a big- band hit.

Alone in his little bedroom over the porch, John dreamed of being somebody—an artist, maybe, or a poet. But after Uncle George got sick and died, John was too sad to dream. All he wanted to do was listen to rock 'n' roll. "Rock 'n' roll was *real*," he said. "Everything else was unreal."

Elvis Presley, Little Richard, Chuck Berry—now *that* was music! John couldn't stop talking about Elvis, whose quivering voice exploded out of the radio in "Heartbreak Hotel."

When Mum saw how much music meant to John, she bought him a cheap guitar and taught him to tune it the only way she knew how— like a banjo. Maybe he could be the Elvis of Liverpool!

John attacked the guitar, strumming as fast as he could. He didn't give a fig about wrong notes. With some of his mates, he organized a skiffle group called the Quarrymen, pounding out souped-up folk songs and some rock 'n' roll. They had no idea how to play, but they loved making noise—*lots* of noise! Rehearsing in Mum's bathroom, the sounds bounced off the tiles. *Bam, BOOM, bam, BOOM!*

Aunt Mimi wouldn't let the boys play at her house. John was supposed to do homework and think about his future. "The guitar's all right for a hobby, John, but you'll never make a living at it," she said.

John didn't believe her. If only he could live with Mum! But all the grown-ups in the family agreed he was better off with Aunt Mimi.

The Quarrymen played one of their gigs on the back of a truck. With his greased-up hair and drainies—tight, skinny jeans that made his legs look like drainpipes—John seemed like a tough Teddy boy, itching for a fight.

Soon they were playing at parties, school dances, and even a real music club, the Cavern. But when the Quarrymen launched into their first song, the manager almost kicked them off the stage. Skiffle groups weren't supposed to play rock 'n' roll!

Some of the boys were ready to quit. Not John. Not when there was one more gig coming up—the St. Peter's Church fair on July 6.

PAUL

Paul McCartney hoped he'd meet some girls at the church fair. Maybe he'd charm them with his long eyelashes. The metal threads of his white jacket winked in the sunlight as he listened to the Quarrymen, and his head bounced to the rhythm. But who was this bloke in the band, and why was he making up new words to "Be-Bop-a-Lula"?

Later, Paul borrowed a guitar and played a few songs for John. Whoa! John was impressed. This kid was only fifteen, but he could tune a guitar properly—*and* he looked like Elvis!

In 1957, Paul lived with his younger brother and their dad in a neat brick house just a mile from John's. Music flowed through every room—show tunes and pop songs on the piano, records on the phonograph, and the constant radio. Dad always pointed out the harmony, chords, and instruments so that Paul would learn to hear music from the inside out. For Paul's thirteenth birthday, Dad had even given him a trumpet.

Paul often biked along the river, where seagulls circled and shrieked. He loved the hustle-bustle down at the docks, where burly men unloaded cargo and tall cranes poked into the sky. When he was in a quiet mood, he sketched, or sat in the woods and read. When he was *not* in a quiet mood, he and his brother threw turnips at passing trains.

Paul had been a good student, but after his mum died of an illness, it was harder to concentrate on schoolwork. His grades went down, down, down.

With Mum gone, Paul felt empty inside. Music helped—especially rock 'n' roll. Lying in bed at night, he slipped on his earphones and tuned in *Saturday Night Jamboree* on the radio. As if in another world, he grooved to the sound of rhythm and blues and bopped to the beat of rock 'n' roll: Fats Domino, Ray Charles, Buddy Holly, Bill Haley, the Everly Brothers—and Elvis, of course. Eventually Paul traded in his trumpet for a guitar. From then on, his brother said, "he didn't have time to eat or think about anything else."

Soon after meeting John, Paul joined the Quarrymen. The two boys took the bus to Paul's house after school, where they snacked on fried eggs or a can of beans, washed down with tea. Then they sat facing each other on the couch, "just bashing away" on their guitars.

Sometimes they wrote songs together, scribbling the words in an old school notebook. Most of the time they tried to imitate the hard-driving songs on the radio. If only the Quarrymen could shake up a room like that! If only they could figure out the chords!

GEORGE

George Harrison was just fourteen in 1957, but he and fifteen-year-old Paul were friends. Both of them were *crazy* for the guitar. When Paul invited George to hear the Quarrymen, he jumped at the chance.

Wow! Paul was right—that John Lennon fellow could *rock*!

Back home, George hunched over his guitar strings, working out the chord changes for Lonnie Donegan's "Rock Island Line," the fingering to songs like "Raunchy," and the twangy country licks in Carl Perkins' "Blue Suede Shoes."

At suppertime, there wasn't much to eat, but there was plenty of laughter. Afterward, George would go to his room, maybe put on a new set of guitar strings, and polish his guitar until it gleamed.

At school, George sat in the back and drew pictures of guitars. But when it came to practicing, no one was more serious. Other kids wanted to just *play* the guitar. "George was out to conquer it," said a friend.

With his big ears and mischievous grin, George worked as a delivery boy on Saturdays, earning money to buy records. Dad wanted him to be an electrician, but George had only one thing on his mind—rock 'n' roll. He'd hear a song a couple times on the radio and—presto!—he could play it perfectly. That boy was made for music!

George played better than any of the Quarrymen, even Paul. He began showing up at their gigs, guitar in hand. John, being two and a half years older, didn't pay much attention.

One February night in 1958, George pulled out his guitar on the top of a double-decker bus and played "Raunchy" for John and Paul. John had to admit that the skinny kid was good—and he knew a *lot* of chords. With George on lead guitar, there'd be no stopping the Quarrymen. He was in.

"Now there were three of us who thought the same," said John.

FORGING A BAND

Whenever John and Paul learned a new chord from George, they'd write a new song. The three friends had electric guitars now, and their playing was getting better all the time.

Then, in the summer of 1958, John's mum was hit by a car and died.

Bitter and angry, John dressed even more like a tough Teddy boy and grew long "sidies," or sideburns. But clothes and hair couldn't hide his unhappiness. Nothing cheered him up, and his funny jokes turned mean.

A gloomy year crawled by. Sometimes the Quarrymen performed; mostly they scrounged for work. John talked his best mate from art college, Stuart Sutcliffe, into playing bass guitar with the band. Stu looked cool, but he couldn't play to save his life.

The boys had so little money that their shoes were full of holes. Without proper equipment, they had to tie their microphones to broomsticks, which their girlfriends held up while they played. On late nights at the Jacaranda coffee bar, they wondered how they'd ever make a living. Sharing an order of toast, they'd argue about the extra penny for jam.

For months, the boys fiddled with the name of the band, finally settling on the Beatles, spelled with an "a." That's when a stroke of luck landed them a gig in Hamburg, Germany. Scraping together some money, they bought matching outfits and pointy winklepicker shoes, hired a drummer named Pete Best, and off they went.

Downtown Hamburg throbbed with noise and neon lights as their van rolled through. The boys were jumping out of their seats with excitement . . . until they saw the Indra club, where they were supposed to play. It was nothing but a dingy bar! And instead of a glamorous hotel to sleep in, they were shown to a couple of cold, smelly rooms in the back of an old movie theater. With their dusty concrete walls, low ceilings, and one small window, the rooms looked, and felt, like jail cells.

"Dungeons," Paul spat.

During their first performances, the nervous boys stood stiffly onstage. *Mach Schau!* the club manager yelled. "Make a show!"

So John began to prance and dance. Paul pretended his guitar was a sword and started "fencing" with John. The boys played faster and cranked up the volume. Loud, LOUD, *LOUD!*

Before long, people were pouring into the club. Hour after hour, night after night, the Beatles worked the crowd into a frenzy with songs like "Good Golly Miss Molly," "Whole Lotta Shakin' Goin' On," and "Great Balls of Fire." The Germans went wild!

When a neighbor complained about the noise, the Beatles were moved to a different club. Then the police found out that George was only seventeen and sent him back to England. Paul and Pete were sent back, too, and John slunk home after them. For a few weeks they didn't even speak to each other. John thought it might be the end of the band.

But it wasn't.

When the Beatles got together again, Liverpool audiences couldn't believe their ears. In Germany, those scruffy English boys had learned how to whip up a room to fever pitch. Soon girls were chasing them down the street for an autograph or a kiss, and teenagers were lining the sidewalk outside the Cavern Club, where rock 'n' roll was now all the rage. Downstairs in the grungy cellar, the Beatles banged out American hits and old favorites. Before long they'd perform more and more of John and Paul's own originals, *Lennon-McCartney* songs. The shows were rough and raw, the noise deafening. It was so hot, even the walls dripped with sweat.

Within months, the Beatles had a fan club and a manager. By then Stu had dropped out, and Paul had taken over on bass guitar. Their new manager, Brian Epstein, dressed them in suits, taught them how to bow, got them an audition with a record company, and laid down some new rules: no more eating, drinking, or swearing onstage. From now on they were *professionals*, headed for the big time.

"Where are we going, fellas?" John would shout.

"To the top, Johnny!" they answered.

"What top?" he yelled.

"The toppermost of the poppermost, Johnny!"

But the record company audition went nowhere. "Guitar groups are on the way out," the boys were told. John, Paul, and George wondered if the problem was the drummer—Pete just didn't seem to fit in.

That spring, Brian knocked on the door of every record company in London. The answer was always the same—no one wanted a bunch of scousers from grimy old Liverpool.

Then the boys received a telegram. One last record producer was willing to hear them play.

On June 6, the Beatles recorded four songs at Abbey Road Studios in London. The producer, Mr. Martin, liked the boys, especially their wisecracking jokes. John, Paul, and George felt they were on the brink of something big. But it was time for a different drummer. And the three friends knew exactly who they wanted.

RINGO

Boom, bop-bop, boom, BOP. Boom, bop-bop, boom, BOP.

Ringo Starr rode those drums like a cowboy on a bucking bronco.

He'd come a long way from the Dingle, the poor, rough neighborhood in the center of Liverpool where he'd grown up an only child, playing in the rubble of bombed-out buildings. His name had been Richard Starkey then.

Little Richy was three years old when his dad left the family and Mum went back to work as a barmaid. Luckily, Grandmum and Grandad lived nearby and helped out.

With his two best mates, Richy liked to roller-skate, swap toys, and play at being the Three Musketeers, cowboys, or detectives. Sometimes they'd set up a "zoo" in the backyard, trapping a spider in a jar and charging a halfpenny for a peek.

Not long before his seventh birthday, Richy's appendix burst. He spent a whole year in the hospital. Being sick was no fun, but he was an easygoing lad and didn't seem to mind.

When Richy was thirteen, Mum remarried. His stepfather was a gentle man who made him laugh, brought him comic books and toys, and encouraged him to listen to music.

Soon after the wedding, Richy came down with a lung disease and was sent to a children's sanatorium for two years. To other boys, this might have felt like a jail sentence. Richy just made friends with the nurses. Best of all, there was a hospital band for patients. That's when he fell in love with the drums.

Back home, Richy couldn't stop his hands from tapping. Listening to all kinds of music—country and western, jazz, blues, skiffle—he'd rap on the back of a chair, bang on a box, or pound an old bass drum with a piece of firewood. "Sometimes, he just slapped a biscuit tin with some keys," said a friend.

Richy loved to dance and was a smart dresser, too. He and his friend went to the Cavern Club in matching outfits and thought themselves "the bee's knees."

Old enough to work, Richy found a steady factory job. With some mates, he started a skiffle group. Then rock 'n' roll hit Liverpool. *Ba-boom, ba-BOOM, ba-boom, ba-BOOM.* Richy's drumming picked up a mean backbeat. By the summer of 1960, he'd quit his job to become a professional musician.

"Drums are my life," he told his family. He tried some different looks and wore a fistful of rings. And he gave himself a new name— Ringo Starr.

Of all the drummers in Liverpool, Ringo was tops. With his beard and his shiny Zephyr Zodiac sports car, he seemed very grown up to John, Paul, and George.

"The beard will have to go," John told Ringo, "but you can keep your sidies."

With his ready, steady beat, Ringo fit in perfectly. His sense of humor matched theirs, too. When asked about his rings, he'd say he wore them on his fingers because he couldn't fit them through his nose!

It was August 18, 1962, and the Beatles were complete.

A few weeks later, John, Paul, George, and Ringo cut their first original record, "Love Me Do." When George first heard it on the radio, he "went shivery all over."

On the road day and night, crisscrossing England, performing at bigger and bigger theaters—sometimes two shows a day—John, Paul, George, and Ringo became close friends. Everywhere they went, girls *screamed* with excitement. The screams became even louder when their second record, "Please Please Me," became a number one hit on the British pop charts.

Soon the Beatles were dubbed the Fab Four. In October 1963, some 15 million people watched them on British television. In November, they performed for royalty.

"BEATLEMANIA!" shouted the newspaper. "You have to be a real sour square not to love the nutty, noisy, happy, handsome Beatles."

Before long, people all over the world fell in love with the lads from Liverpool. Some thought success had come overnight to John, Paul, George, and Ringo. But those who knew them saw that their success grew out of childhood dreams—the dreams of kids who first heard rock 'n' roll through the crackle and buzz of cheap transistor radios and were electrified by the red-hot sound.

Those boys had poured hundreds of hours of sweat, love, and teenage energy into their music. Their songs were irresistible, and they were the best of friends.

That friendship cast a spell across the globe. The Beatles' days in the spotlight had just begun.

THE BEATLES

AUTHOR'S NOTE

I discovered the Beatles in 1964, when they appeared on the *Ed Sullivan* television show during their first trip to the United States. Still too young to buy records, I pored over their photos in *Life* magazine while my parents muttered disapproving comments about their long hair. I decided that Paul was my favorite. That year, the band had six number one hits in the United States, and Beatles songs became the defining sound track of my childhood.

Half a century later, the Fab Four and their music continue to foster fierce loyalty and debate among fans. Thousands of books, articles, films, and websites provide information—and misinformation—about the band, and their songs are known and loved by billions. Yet most people know little about the boys who became the Beatles.

In writing this book, I wanted to show how four ordinary boys growing up amid the rubble of postwar Liverpool found music to be a powerful, even life-saving, force in their lives. The challenge was to weave together the lives of four individuals—each with a unique family history—and the story of the band they created. With so much material available, I had to make difficult choices about which fascinating facts and witty quotes to include. For example, did you know that when the Beatles were boys, milk was still delivered by horse-drawn cart and only the McCartneys had a telephone? That John's aunt Mimi called Paul "your little friend"? That Ringo liked being in the hospital because he got to have butter on his bread? "A dollop of butter was big news in those days," he said. For readers who would like to learn more, a treasure trove awaits.

"I believe that you actually feel the love in the craft,
in the art, from the four individuals who were there.
There was really a very strong bond, and I don't think you can
make music like that without that bond."
—RINGO STARR

GLOSSARY

BACKBEAT. A rhythmic accent on the second and fourth beats of a four-beat musical measure, typical of rock 'n' roll.

BLOKE. A man.

COUNTRY LICK. An instrumental phrase in country and western music, usually played on solo guitar.

DRUM FILL. A brief rhythmic passage that fills the time between sections of a song.

GIG. A job, for musicians.

GUITAR RIFF. A short repeated musical phrase played on the guitar.

LAD. A boy or young man.

PHONOGRAPH. A record player.

SANATORIUM. An institution for people with chronic diseases.

SCOUSERS. People from Liverpool, named after a popular local dish called *scouse*, a kind of stew; also known as Liverpudlians.

SKIFFLE. A form of folk music with jazz, blues, and country influences that uses homemade instruments such as washboard and thimble, tea-chest bass, and cigar-box fiddle, along with acoustic guitar or banjo.

TEDDY BOY. Tough young men in 1950s England who dressed in knee-length jackets with velvet or satin collars, narrow pants, white shirts, fancy vests, and skinny "Slim Jim" ties; a style named for clothes worn during the reign of King Edward VII, or "Teddy."

NOTES

"There is such a thing as magic," Paul McCartney, quoted in *Rolling Stone*, May 3, 2007, 61.

"Give me a squeaker," Spitz, 32.

"Rock 'n' roll was *real*," John Lennon, quoted in *The Beatles Anthology*, 11.

"The guitar's all right for a hobby," Mimi Smith, quoted by John Lennon in *The Beatles Anthology*, 11.

"He didn't have time to eat," Michael McCartney, quoted in Davies, 31.

"just bashing away," Paul McCartney, quoted in Spitz, 110.

"George was out to conquer it," Colin Manley, quoted in Spitz, 123.

"Now there were three of us," John Lennon, quoted in Davies, 45.

"Dungeons," Paul McCartney, quoted in Pawlowski, 25.

"*Mach Schau!*" Wilhelm Limpensel, quoted by John Lennon in *The Beatles Anthology*, 47.

"Where are we going, fellas?" John Lennon quoted by George Harrison in Davies, 132.

"Guitar groups are on the way out," George Harrison, quoted in *The Beatles Anthology*, 67.

"Sometimes, he just slapped a biscuit tin," Roy Trafford, quoted in Spitz, 341.

"the bee's knees," ibid., 343.

"Drums are my life," Ringo Starr, quoted in *The Beatles Anthology*, 38.

"The beard will have to go," John Lennon, quoted in Miles, 90.

"went shivery all over," George Harrison, quoted in Davies, 163.

"BEATLEMANIA!" *Daily Mirror*, November 5, 1963, quoted in Norman, 221.

"your little friend," Mimi Smith quoted by Paul McCartney in Miles, 44.

"A dollop of butter," Ringo Starr, quoted in *The Beatles Anthology*, 35.

"I believe that you actually feel the love," Ringo Starr, quoted in *Rolling Stone*, op. cit., 67.

SOURCES

BOOKS AND ARTICLES

The Beatles. *The Beatles Anthology*. San Francisco: Chronicle Books, 2000.

Coleman, Ray. *Lennon*. New York: McGraw-Hill, 1984.

Davies, Hunter. *The Beatles*. 2nd revised edition. New York: McGraw-Hill, 1985.

DeCurtis, Anthony. "Paul McCartney." *Rolling Stone* 40th Anniversary Issue. May 3, 2007.

———. "Ringo Starr." *Rolling Stone* 40th Anniversary Issue. May 3, 2007.

Harrison, George. *I Me Mine*. New York: Chronicle, 2002.

Lewisohn, Mark. *The Complete Beatles Chronicle*. New York: Harmony Books, 1992.

———. *Tune In: The Beatles: All These Years*, Volume 1. New York: Crown Archetype, 2013.

Miles, Barry. *Paul McCartney: Many Years from Now*. New York: Henry Holt and Company, 1997.

Norman, Philip. *Shout!: The Beatles in Their Generation*. Revised edition. New York: Simon & Schuster, 2005.

Partridge, Elizabeth. *John Lennon: All I Want Is the Truth*. New York: Viking, 2005.

Pawlowski, Garth L. *How They Became The Beatles*. New York: E.P. Dutton, 1989.

Pritchard, David, and Alan Lysaght. *The Beatles: An Oral History*. New York: Hyperion, 1998.

Spitz, Bob. *The Beatles: The Biography*. New York: Little, Brown and Company, 2005.

FILMS, VIDEOS, AND DVDS

Beat City. An Associated-Rediffusion Production, 1963.

The Beatles: A Long and Winding Road. Passport Entertainment, 2003.

The Beatles Anthology. Produced by Neil Aspinall, Chips Chipperfield, Stan Storc, 1996.

The Compleat Beatles. Produced by Delilah Films and released by MGM/UA, 1984.

WEBSITES

beatlesagain.com

brianepstein.com

cavernclub.org/history

georgeharrison.com

johnlennon.com

liverpoolbeatlescene.com

liverpoolmuseums.org.uk/wml/exhibitions/thebeatgoeson

originalquarrymen.co.uk

paulmccartney.com

petebest.com

ringostarr.com

thebeatles.com

triumphpc.com/mersey-beat

To Mike McCoy, Fab Friend

—S. R.

For Noah and Adrian

—A. G.

Henry Holt and Company, LLC
Publishers since 1866
175 Fifth Avenue
New York, New York 10010
mackids.com

Library of Congress Cataloging-in-Publication Data
Reich, Susanna, author.
Fab four friends : the boys who became the Beatles / Susanna Reich ; illustrated by Adam Gustavson.
pages   cm
ISBN 978-0-8050-9458-9 (hardcover)
1. Beatles—Juvenile literature. 2. Rock musicians—England—Biography—Juvenile literature.
I. Gustavson, Adam, illustrator. II. Title.
ML3930.B39R45 2015   782.42166092'2—dc23   [B]   2014042068

Henry Holt books may be purchased for business or promotional use. For information on
bulk purchases, please contact the Macmillan Corporate and Premium Sales Department at
(800) 221-7945 x5442 or by e-mail at specialmarkets@macmillan.com.

First Edition—2015 / Designed by Patrick Collins
The artist used oil paint on prepared paper to create the illustrations for this book.
Printed in China by R. R. Donnelley Asia Printing Solutions Ltd., Dongguan City, Guangdong Province

1 3 5 7 9 10 8 6 4 2